BENT BUT NOT BROKEN

HELP AND HOPE FOR MARRIAGE RESTORATION

Gerald and Yvette Benton

Copyright © 2020 Gerald and Yvette Benton.

All rights reserved, no portion of this book may be reproduced, photocopied, stored or transmitted in any form -except by prior approval of the author or the publisher, except as permitted by U.S. copyright law.

Printed by

Gerald and Yvette Ministries

Kennesaw, GA

Amplified Bible (AMP)

Copyright © 2015 by The Lockman Foundation, La Habra, CA 90631. All rights reserved.

Amplified Bible, Classic Edition (AMPC)

Copyright © 1954, 1958, 1962, 1964, 1965, 1987 by The Lockman Foundation

Scripture quotations are taken from the King James Version of the Bible.

Benton, Yvette. HELP FOR THE HELPMEET: GOD'S STRATEGIES FOR BECOMING HIS HELPMEET SUITABLE. Kennesaw, GA: Help For The Helpmeet, Inc, 2019.

Printed in the United States of America

U.S. Copyright No. Pending

ISBN: 978-1-7346335-0-4

Acknowledgments

A very special thank you to Jasma Starks and Dr. Katrina Foster for their labor of love and hard work to help us birth this vision. We love you both so much!

Dedication

Yvette, as I was reading our story, I began to cry tears of joy and happiness. God showed me a long time ago what it would look like to love again, but I had no idea that it would look like this. You have truly been a gift from God for me. You are my heart and I thank God for you. I thank you Father for keeping your promise to a man that was broken but now healed to love again. I'm so grateful to have my best friend back.

    Love, Your King Gerald

    Gerald, I've known you for 35 years. Some years were good, some not so good. As I reflect on our story, I can truly say that I love you more now than I've ever loved you before. The God in you makes the "not so good years" a faint memory! I have my best friend back! Thank you!

    Love, Your Helpmeet Suitable Yvette

Table of Contents

Introduction 1
The Love Story 1
Chapter 1 7
God Had Plans For You Before You Were Born 7
Chapter 2 16
What You May Think Is The Right Path May Not Be The Case 16
Chapter 3 25
Are You Equipped To Take The Right Path? 25
Chapter 4 33
Why Did You Take Us Down This Road? 33
Chapter 5 42
The Turn-Around 42
Chapter 6 52
Redeeming The Time 52
Chapter 7 59
Living Life On The Path God Chose From The Beginning 59
LETTER TO HELPMEETS 68
YVETTE BENTON 68
Help Insert From Help For The Helpmeet 76
Introduction 77
Chapter 1 79
I Want To Be A Helpmeet 79

Chapter 2 85
Helpmeet The Hardest Job With No Training 85
RESTORATION 95
Chapter 1 96
Restoration Is Possible 96
Restoration Prayer 102

Introduction

The Love Story

The Beginning

Gerald and Yvette met in high school. Although Gerald was a newly transferred Freshman to the school, he was bold enough to walk up to Yvette, who was a Junior, and declare, "I don't know who you are, but I'm going to marry you someday." This was the beginning of a very close friendship. Although Gerald never stopped pursuing Yvette romantically, Yvette always insisted they would remain strictly platonic friends. Gerald was a star football player, and Yvette a cheerleader. They were inseparable until the day Yvette decided to enroll in a college in another state. Gerald was devastated, and the two lost touch.

The Fairytale

Just as any great love story would have it, Gerald and Yvette found their way back together. Eleven years had passed, and Yvette had moved back to their hometown in Florida to work as a Guidance Counselor at the same high school she and Gerald met. Gerald had enjoyed a successful career as a football player at both the college and professional levels and was working as a College Football Coach in Kansas. As only God could do, Gerald was assigned to recruit a football player from his alma mater. He called the school to get information on the athlete. When he called the school, he was transferred to the Guidance department, and Yvette answered the phone. The two were both shocked to hear the other's voice, and they began to reminisce. A few months later, Gerald called his grandmother's home, and Yvette's sister happened to be there visiting her friend, who was also Gerald's cousin. Gerald knew this was another sign and asked her for Yvette's phone number. By then, he said, "I'm not waiting any longer; it's time for Yvette and me to get it together." Six months later after a long-distance courtship, they were married. Everyone thought it was the most beautiful true love story.

The Shift

After about five years of marriage, Gerald and Yvette were both growing spiritually and began taking on leadership roles at their church. The church started moving in the Apostolic, and the teaching became focused on deliverance and holiness. With that shift, Yvette's prophetic and discernment gifts were developing, and she began to see various concerns regarding Gerald's lifestyle. He had secretly been addicted to pornography and drugs. As they attended conferences and trainings, Gerald was blessed to get deliverance, and they both felt this was the beginning of their ministry together. However, Satan had other plans. Gerald slowly slipped back into his old ways, lies began to be told, jobs were lost, and the marriage suffered. The family almost lost their home to foreclosure several times, and the two were going in separate directions spiritually. Gerald was dealing with generational curses of lust and perversion, along with rebellion, bitterness, and a lying spirit. He refused to change, and the two eventually separated. At that point, Gerald was homeless or living in his truck, sleeping at relative's homes. He was lost. Eventually, he swallowed his pride and moved back home, promising to change, only for the two to argue and become more distant. The changes were short-lived. Yvette blamed Gerald for their financial struggles, although her career was thriving. After two separations, Yvette attended a church service, and during the message, God spoke to her and said, "If Satan came into your home and took your son, Jordan, would you let him?" Of course, her answer was, "NO!" God quickly replied, "Well, Satan came into your home and took Gerald, and you didn't do anything about it, and he's MY SON!" After that day, Yvette repented and decided to fight. Not so much for the marriage, but out of obedience to God and for Gerald's salvation and deliverance.

Sanctified Wife

After seeking God's direction, Yvette was determined to do what most thought was not only impossible but crazy. She began to forgive her husband and work on herself! She asked God what He wanted from her, and He led her to pray for her own deliverance. This led to the beginning of her journey to becoming a Helpmeet suitable. She began realizing that she had not honored Gerald as the Bible says or forgiven him as she should. Although his behavior and habits weren't Godly, God's Word required her to respect and be obedient. Yvette learned to treat him like she had never been hurt. They reconciled, and Gerald could see and feel the presence of God in their home and in the way Yvette was loving him unconditionally. The atmosphere of their home was conducive for deliverance, and the power of God transformed Gerald's life. He began his deliverance process, and he could trust Yvette with his darkest secrets and fears because she had proven that she was not giving up on him.

God's Restoration Power

As God delivered Gerald from generational curses, pains of the past, and addictions, He also began restoring their marriage. The two are now becoming one, as the Bible says, and they are sharing their life and testimony with others to provide help and hope. They remind people through their ministry that "marriage works if you work it!" Gerald and Yvette now travel as representatives for Derek Prince Ministries, teach marriage seminars, provide online counseling and mentoring, while also ministering on social media outlets and at churches. Their online broadcast covers topics to help marriages grow, thrive, and restore. The broadcasts are "Marriage Workouts" at the GYM (Gerald and Yvette Ministries). They are truly living the life that God intended for them to live as overcomers by the words of their testimony. God can, and He will restore!

Come on a journey with Gerald and Yvette as they tell their story of how God restored them both individually and then their marriage. Gerald will share his testimony and what it took for him to get free and stay free. Yvette will share with you the process and strategies God gave her to heal, pray, and declare over Gerald. This is a message of help and hope. Get ready for God to blow your mind!

HOPE

GERALD BENTON

Chapter 1

God Had Plans For You Before You Were Born

"For I know the plans and thoughts that I have for you, says the LORD. Plans for peace and well-being and not for disaster, to give you a future and a hope." JEREMIAH 29:11 (AMP)

Have you ever wondered where your father was? I pose this question because I wondered the same thing growing up. This was a missing piece to the puzzle in my life—a piece I so desperately needed. It seemed like the men in my neighborhood would fulfill that role in my eyes, but of course, only to a certain extent. My childhood neighborhood had a local store on the corner where older men would gather in the mornings. At the age of five, I would wake up early to meet them there. As time went on, they began to call me "Right On," which meant right on time. These neighborhood men watched over me as a father would do. They made sure I was ok and went to school daily. This was the support of male figures in my life. But, when I saw my friends with their fathers, it made me wonder even more about this missing piece in my life- my own father. My mother and grandmother raised me, so I grew up in a single-parent home. My father was around, but he was not in my day-to-day life, and there was a void that was not being fulfilled. This just added to the various emotional problems my mother dealt with consistently.

My mother and my grandfather didn't get along. He spoke things over my mother that Satan used to try to alter her and my destiny. His words spoke to her seed, which was me. My mother had me before she left for college, and her father told her she wouldn't be anything in life, and her life was messed up because she had me early. Because my father was not in the picture, it made it seem like I was the problem. At the age of three, my mother left me with my aunt and grandmother while she went to school for physical education. I didn't know any better or understand the depth of my mother's decision to leave me. At that point, I didn't live with either of my biological parents. But, when I look back on that decision, I realize that it changed my life. This was the beginning of the thoughts of suicide. This spirit was able to creep in through the rejection I was feeling from my parents. I would always say, "Why can't I have a mom and dad at my house?" I felt rejected and unwanted. Feelings a child shouldn't have to feel at such a young age. I was now living with a hurt grandmother, who had just divorced my grandfather. I loved my grandmother; she did a great job of doing what she knew to do with me. But, in retrospect, she didn't know how to love because of the hurt she was going through.

When my mom was away in college, I would visit her here and there. At that time, I wasn't connected to my mom because I lived with my grandmother. When my mom finished college and moved back home, I was about six years old. I still stayed with my grandmother for a while though my mom went on to have three more sons out of wedlock. I felt more abandoned because they had her attention—the attention that I didn't receive at a young age. The decision that my mother made to leave and the rejection I felt took a long time for me to get over. I battled with this for years and continue to work through it.

When I did go to my mother's house and live with her, the situation was no better because she worked overnight shifts, and that meant I needed a babysitter. I had no idea this babysitter would ultimately bring destruction into my life. She planted a seed that would distort my thinking, my perspective of love, and it would ultimately feed spirits of rejection and emptiness. One day out of the blue, my babysitter stated, "I am going to show you what love is." At the age of 6 or 7, I didn't know any better. I didn't know what genuine love meant or felt like because I had so many missing pieces in my life. My high school-aged babysitter would tell me to go to the bathroom and take a shower. She would come into the bathroom and say, "Let me wash your back." "Let me touch you." She would fondle with my private area, and once I got aroused, she would say, "That's a sign of love." After we got out of the shower, she would fondle herself and expose me to her most intimate body parts. She would lay my head on her breasts and tell me where to put my fingers on her body and mine. She taught me how to masturbate. Therefore, as a young boy, perversion was planted into my mind and heart as love. These acts carried on for a year or so. My expression of love was to act out sexually. Being exposed so young opened other doors for pornography (which were pornographic magazines) back in the day. When looking at these magazines with friends and alone, we would begin to fantasize about different women and describe what we would "do" to these women. In addition, my mom had a homosexual friend that touched me and kissed me on the neck but didn't go much farther. Most likely because I elbowed him to getaway! There were also moments when I would walk through the house, and various family members would be having sex and I could hear them because they left their doors open. There were also times I would stand or sit at the door listening and masturbate. The mental picture of these acts was imprinted in my mind.

This is love, right?

That's what the babysitter taught me. I never spoke of what the babysitter did to me. My mother knew nothing of what happened. I was so bound in lust, perversion, and sexual sins. These spirits had a strong influence over me. At the age I was, I knew it wasn't right to keep a secret, but I had no idea how these acts would affect my life or whether it was right or wrong. I walked heavily in this sin, and it grew with me for years.

I can tell you this story now because I am unashamed and delivered from what was planted as a child. This foundation had to be laid as you walk with me through my journey in this book. A seed of perversion was unfortunately planted (as is the case for many), but there is freedom. Through deliverance, I began to remember what happened to me because the memories were suppressed in my mind. So many people have been molested, fondled, and/or sexually assaulted as a child. Very often, the person committing the act was a victim themselves. This in no way excuses the violation, but it shows the setup from the enemy to hinder multiple destinies. This demonic assignment is often kept a secret due to shame and embarrassment. If you are reading this book, and you have been a victim of molestation, please find a trusted individual to seek Godly counsel. It should be one who understands and is knowledgeable in healing and deliverance. This will be the beginning of your freedom from the trap of perversion.

You may think your life is over, and you're trapped. The devil is a liar! Continue reading and watch how Holy Spirit opens your eyes to the tricks of the enemy. From the very beginning, the enemy knew God had a plan for my life, and his primary assignment was to destroy me. The same is for you. The plan of the enemy is terminated today. Satan uses people, places, and things to plant seeds. God's Word says that He has a plan for me and you. The missing pieces of my father and mother opened the door and gave access to the illegal spirits that operated in my life. Bloodline and generational curses played a huge role in trying to stop God's plans for me. There are always roots to these curses, and many root issues stem from childhood. Let's stay in this vein as we move to the next chapter.

Gerald's Prayer

Lord, thank You for delivering me from perversion, molestation, and generational curses that were passed down through my bloodline. Father, I forgive anyone who has hurt me and caused trauma in my life. Allow others to forgive me for the trauma I caused as well. Father, I thank You for the plans and the people You have placed in my life to help me. Thank You for every man who made an impact on my life because my father was absent. You have always been my father, and You are a father to the fatherless. Thank You for Your patience with me to allow me to find my way back from hell into the path You had initially designed for me. I submit and humble myself to Your will for my life. I choose Your plan over my plan and Your will over my will. Lord, I speak deliverance over my soul. Your Word says that You order the steps of a righteous man. Lord, order my steps so that I will walk out the plans You have for me righteously every day.

In Jesus' name, Amen.

Reflections

Have you ever been violated in your childhood? Cancel those experiences off of your life and cry out to God for deliverance.

_____
_____
_____
_____
_____
_____
_____
_____
_____
_____
_____
_____
_____
_____
_____
_____

Reflections

Chapter 2

What You May Think Is The Right Path May Not Be The Case

"Abandoning the straight road [that is, the right way to live], they have gone astray; they have followed the way of [the false teacher] Balaam the son of Beor, who loved the reward of wickedness." 2 PETER 2:15 (AMP)

Going to church was a must in my household. My mother and grandmother made sure I went. Every Sunday, we were in church, as my bloodline had generations of preachers. My grandfather preached all his life, and his dad was a preacher and started a church in the early fifties. So, you could say I was born to do the will of God, be a man of God, and to make an impact on my generation by preaching the Word of God. Jeremiah 1:5 states, "Before I formed thee in the belly, I knew thee, and before thou camest forth out of the womb, I sanctified thee, and I ordained thee a prophet unto the nations" (KJV). As I got older, there were more and more preachers on my mother's side of the family. My mother became a preacher, and so did my aunt and several uncles. Most of my grandfather's children were preaching the gospel. I actually loved going to church, not knowing that one day, I would be doing the same thing. As an adult, I watched my mother study and live the Bible. My mother began to display an example of a great Christian life. My mother had faith beyond anything I could ever imagine. I watched God work miracles in her life. She would apply the Word to everything. I remember the doctor telling her that she needed a heart transplant and her response to that was, "My God heals." She never got a heart transplant because she believed God for her healing. Watching miracles happen in her life helped me believe God for any and everything. She would say, "Gerald, watch your words because your words are powerful, and people are going to have to believe what you're speaking." I didn't understand what she was talking about. I thought the statement was more geared toward lying. I would often tell her I was going to do something and wouldn't do it. Now that I am a man, I understand what she was talking about and why it hurt her when I wasn't living up to my word, for Ephesians 4:29 says, "Let no corrupt communication proceed out of your mouth, but that which is good to the use of edifying, that it may minister grace unto the hearers."

My mother saw my destiny and what I was going to need to fulfill it; she also knew the other side of preaching based on my family member's lifestyles. Some preached the Word and lived a different life than what they preached. This was a bloodline and generational curse that hindered me. My mother saw how my grandfather misused the Word. This was a seed planted as well: it was okay to do the Lord's work while fulfilling the lusts of the flesh. As we discussed sexual sin in the first chapter, this was also a generational curse in my bloodline. Not to disrespect, but honestly, my mother had me out of wedlock, my grandfather had children out of wedlock, committed adultery, and several family members were having sex without concern about what I saw or knew. The sin continued to be passed down from generation to generation.

As time moved forward, before I was delivered from lust and perversion, I married my high school sweetheart. I'm sure you can imagine the problems I brought into the marriage. As a married man with a family that appeared to be fully committed to a church, God had given me an understanding of the call on my life and the great destiny that He had for me. A great Apostle came to our church and spoke a profound prophetic word over my life that I could not understand at the time. The word was "weighty", and I felt unworthy of the call. I would ask myself, "Why me?" God would say, "Why not you!" I thought about my family misusing their power within the church. I feared I would also operate in this generational curse. I was so frightened that I ran from the word that was spoken over my life for a long time. If you know God and have a relationship with Him, you know that you can only run from Him for so long. You can't run from the call that's on your life. You can try, but the misery that comes with not fulfilling your call is not something you want to live with. I would see the gifts that God placed in me. I knew what I operated in, and it flowed so naturally through me. By this time, my wife had been preaching for a while. She understood God's standards and order. She would not lower them for anything, not even me. I didn't understand my wife at this time. It was a big problem because I knew I had gifts and a calling for my life, but I wanted to operate in my gifts and still live a sinful lifestyle.

Romans 11:29 says, "For the gifts and calling of God are without repentance."

My wife was not having this at all. It pushed our relationship to the point that I left home and the church. It was like I had one foot in and one foot out. I would come home at times on fire for God, but it didn't last long. At that time, I just wanted to be seen. It was a selfish agenda. I wanted to be seen as a preacher, but not live by the standards of God or to be held accountable. That's what I saw growing up, so why not? No one seemed to check the way they were living outside the church. Out of my mouth, I would always say I didn't want to live my life as my grandfather did, but I was doing the same thing. I tried to live out 1 Corinthians 9:27, which says, "But I keep under my body, and bring it into subjection: lest that by any means, when I have preached to others, I should be a castaway" (KJV).

Once again, the devil was trying to stop my destiny. I believe wholeheartedly that my grandfather was limited in ministry because of his lifestyle. If he had lived a lifestyle that God was pleased with, he could have reached many more people. I am a fourth generational preacher with a calling more significant than I can comprehend. This is great indeed, but I could not break the strongholds on my life that were formed from generational curses and some I caused by my decisions. I knew what the Word said about living a righteous and holy lifestyle, but the life I lived was way off the path God called me to walk down. My thought pattern was that how I am living is okay; I'm not hurting anyone. Or so I thought. The devil had a stronghold on my thought life. It was a road that he set up for me, a dark road to keep me from reaching my destiny. I desired to have things come easily and quickly for me. I was truly deceived. Deuteronomy 11:16 says, "Take heed to yourselves, that your heart is not deceived, and ye turn aside, and serve other gods, and worship them" (KJV). Don't let your heart deceive you and your family. I desired to do the will of God, but I was so bound I didn't know how to get free, so I continued in my sin. That was all I knew. Everything that was planted at a young age and the generational curses that surfaced when I acted out affected my life and my family.

I was also skilled and gifted in the area of football. Being on the field was my safe place, but off the field, I was faced with the same reality of the things I tried to get away from. It seemed like in every new area or stage in my life, I dealt with bondage. As you're reading this, Holy Spirit may be revealing your own generational curses to you. You may also be gifted in a specific area of your life and use it to try to escape your present reality. Let's look at my life of football.

Gerald's Prayer

Father, Your Word says in Isaiah 54:17, "No weapon formed against me shall prosper, and every tongue which rises up against me in judgment shall be condemned," and this is my inheritance in the Lord. Right now, I condemn every negative word that has been spoken over myself, my family, and my future in Jesus' name. Father, I embrace the call on my life. Do with me as you see fit. I was bought with a price, and Father, I thank you for what Your Son did for me on the cross.

In Jesus' name, Amen.

Reflections

Are there generational curses that have attempted to alter the call of God on your or your spouse's life?

_____
_____
_____
_____
_____
_____
_____
_____
_____
_____
_____
_____
_____
_____
_____
_____

Reflections

Chapter 3

Are You Equipped To Take The Right Path?

"Put on the full armor of God [for His precepts are like the splendid armor of a heavily-armed soldier], so that you may be able to [successfully] stand up against all the schemes and the strategies and the deceits of the devil." EPHESIANS 6:11 (AMP)

As a man, I struggled with identity issues. I knew the call on my life but accepting who I was that was the real battle. Football was my identity for a long time. I lived and breathed football. There was nothing that could compare. I was skilled in playing. The football field was safe from the addictions and my reality. I started playing football at the age of 5 flag football until I was able to play tackle. Football was fun. It was my passion. It was off the field that I was met with my reality again. Sports came easy to me. I was naturally gifted in athletics.

After being successful in high school football, where I played offense, defense and on special teams, I went to college in Kansas on a scholarship. I played at a Junior College before going to a 4-year university. Although I was highly recruited, my grades ultimately hindered me from attending a university after graduation. This was extremely traumatic and caused me to truly suffer from a spirit of failure. I felt like the one area I was successful had been taken from me. I did eventually attend Kansas State University on a football scholarship. After a very successful college career, I reached my goal of playing in the National Football League (NFL) with the Houston Oilers. Following my time there, I played for 2 teams in the Canadian Football League (CFL). During these years, the spirit of perversion within me grew worse. In my view, the men that played professional football were so "free"—free to do drugs, drink alcohol, and use women. Multiple sexual partners was common because a lot of time was spent in nude bars after practice and during travel. I went to the clubs often and participated in these perverse activities for many years. All this did was intensify my cravings and increase my sexual appetite. Conversations in the locker room were a free- for-all and tell it all. All I heard was, "I'm messing with this girl and that girl". The conversations fed the sin and made the cravings undeniably stronger. These cravings I couldn't shake easily.

I played football professionally until I was about 25 years old. It was then that I got injured and had surgery on my knee. There was so much pressure to perform and be on top of my game. I really wasn't prepared mentally to understand the business of football. I played the game of football all I could, then I became tired and told my roommate, "I'm not going to practice anymore." I called my agent and told him I was ready to come back to the States. The Canadian Football League ended for me. The one successful part of my life came to an end. Many professional football players suffer from depression or contemplate suicide because they have no other part of their lives to look forward to after it is over. It was at that point that the spirits of depression and suicide had a mission. They made me feel like there was nothing else to live for, waking up morning after morning in a place of despair. So, I went back to my coping mechanisms—drinking, smoking, watching pornography, and using people. The childhood babysitter planted the seed, and professional football watered it. Being a star football player made it easy for me to get what I wanted. I became very cocky, and the spirit of pride was strong in my life. My thinking allowed me to believe "I'm good," "I can handle this".

As a football player, it is vital to wear football equipment, and if you don't, most likely you will get hurt. In the spirit, it's the same process. We can't play on the field for God without the right uniform. I was losing the battle because I wasn't putting on the right equipment. Ephesians 6:13 says, "Therefore, put on the complete armor of God, so that you will be able to [successfully] resist and stand your ground in the evil day [of danger], and having done everything [that the crisis demands], to stand firm [in your place, fully prepared, immovable, victorious]" (AMP).

Not once did I go on the football field without the right equipment. If I got hit, I would suffer from physical trauma to my body. Yet, I would wake up every morning and not put on my spiritual equipment, which is important also. I heard Ephesians 6:13 numerous times, but I wasn't applying it to my daily life. What a big mistake! I would put on a helmet in football to protect my head while in the game on the field. Why wouldn't I do the same with the helmet of salvation? As I see myself getting dressed, shoulder pads are like the breastplate of righteousness; they protect the heart. You get the picture—protect yourself against the enemy at all times. Naturally, I knew protection when it came to football, but not protecting myself or my family when it came to the schemes of the devil. I was winning in sports but losing in life, the one area in which I was called to have dominion. As a husband, I had no direction, wearing the wrong equipment for the battle I needed to fight. This inconsistency went on for years.

My wife and family were getting battered due to the lack of protection on my part. Then God woke me up and delivered me out of the hands of the enemy, just like in Jeremiah 15:21, "And

I will deliver thee out of the hand of the wicked, and I will redeem thee out of the hand of the terrible" (AMP). God explained to me that His armor was not just for my protection, but the security I needed to win battles for my family. I am the head of my household. I was given the power to be the example of Christ to my family. My assignment is to protect them at all costs. At the time, I was not completing my assignments. We were getting defeated before the game even started. Once I understood why I needed the right equipment on, the score changed. No longer am I losing, but now because of the grace of God, I am a winner, and my family is protected. My thoughts and heart are lined up with God and His Word. I am walking in the right direction and peace that surpasses all understanding. Glory to God for His mercy that has followed me all the days of my life. Remember, every day, you need to put on the armor of God. It will save your life.

Gerald's Prayer

Father, thank You for delivering me from the "I'm good" spirit that had me living a life of lies. Thank You for delivering me from the strongholds of entitlement, lust, perversion, rejection, depression and a generational curse of pride. Jeremiah 15:21 states, "And I will deliver thee out of the hand of the wicked, and I will redeem thee out of the hand of the terrible." Father, You are not a man that You should lie. I believe what Your Word says, and You have truly kept Your Word. Thank You for delivering me out of the hands of the wicked and the hand of terrible. Abba, thank You for loving and seeing the best in me when I couldn't see it for myself.

In Jesus' name, Amen.

Reflections

Are you putting on the whole armor of God? If not, what areas of your life are unprotected?

_____
_____
_____
_____
_____
_____
_____
_____
_____
_____
_____
_____
_____
_____
_____
_____
_____

Reflections

Chapter 4

Why Did You Take Us Down This Road?

"Indeed, we hear that some among you are leading an undisciplined and inappropriate life, doing no work at all, but acting like busybodies [meddling in other people's business]." 2 THESSALONIANS 3:11 (AMP)

As a believer, it is impossible to serve two masters. Matthew 6:24, states, "No one can serve two masters; for either he will hate the one and love the other, or he will be devoted to the one and despise the other. You cannot serve God and mammon [money, possessions, fame, status, or whatever is valued more than the Lord]"(AMP). There were seasons of my life, I tried to serve two masters; God and my flesh. I valued my undisciplined and inappropriate lifestyle more than I valued God, yet still tried to please God. The Bible clearly states that sin is fun for a season (Hebrew 11:25). I was definitely going to make sure I had all the fun before my season ran out. What a joke! It was like I was living a double lifestyle. James 1:18 paints a clear picture of what that means, of "being a double-minded man, unstable and restless in all his ways [in everything he thinks, feels, or decides]." God was not pleased with this type of lifestyle; in fact, he was mad. This lifestyle took my family and me down roads that a man shouldn't want his family to ever have to travel.

I was undisciplined in my relationship with God, marriage, and parenting. I couldn't keep a job to provide for myself, let alone my family. We went through financial and marital struggles. I was undisciplined in all my ways and my thoughts. 1 Timothy 5:8 says, "If anyone fails to provide for his own, and especially for those of his own family, he has denied the faith [by disregarding its precepts] and is worse than an unbeliever [who fulfills his obligation in these matters] (AMP)."

It was a rough time for my family and me. My sins were getting the best of me because of the drug and alcohol addictions, immature behavior and the inappropriate acts of perversion that were driven and produced by the addictions, curses and trauma. It was literally a disaster for all of us. I was particularly bound by pornography, masturbation, and other habits that made being a husband and father almost impossible. I had trustworthy people in my life and received sound advice, but I didn't do what I was told. I became very rebellious. It was easier to keep the cycle going and do what I wanted to do. The shame I was bringing on my wife and family was destructive but, after a while, I honestly didn't care. If you ever looked at my wife, you would not have known we were dealing with these types of problems. We kept everything inside our house. We told a couple of people, but they didn't know how bad things were. We traveled this road for so many years we both became numb. Due to my lack of authority over my life, I lost jobs, friends, and family, and I still didn't change. I was blind, and the devil had me on the road to death and destruction.

My wife wanted to call it quits, get out of the marriage plenty of times, to get off the crazy "ride" we were on. By being the head of the family, I was bringing curses on the family that they didn't deserve. These cycles went on for a long time, off and on for over 10 years. There were times when I was doing great and then ended up back into the same cycle of perverted actions and drug usage. Soul ties, cycles, and generational curses work hand and hand to keep you bound to your past and stop you from moving forward. These very spirits did their job and did it well, unfortunately. My family was hurt and displeased with my lifestyle. They had to think, "Why is he taking us down this road?" "How could he be so selfish?" It's not easy to come out of sin when bound by it. It takes commitment and work to get free and stay free. Soul ties form emotional attachments to people, places, and things. The longer I formed the attachments, the more I fed it. Cycles of sin are destructive habits that are repeated over and over again. Generational curses are passed through bloodlines, and family sins passed down from generations. If these demonic assignments are never broken, the cycles keep going. The goal is to identify the root causes of the cycle and uproot it. My mind and heart wanted to say no, but at the same time, my flesh was causing me to sin. My flesh was stronger than my will. I had no control because, for years, I gave my flesh the right to control my decisions. This is when I would run. I felt I could no longer stay in the home. At times I wanted to be there, because I knew a part of me loved my wife and family, but the torment in my mind was so strong. Every time I tried to stop the habits or behaviors, I would fail. This caused our marriage relationship to become destructive.

We had already separated twice and tried to come back together to work it out. Things were better at first, but we would just end up having the same arguments over and over and I would slowly go back to my habits. The third separation was the longest. I had been fired from my job. I knew Yvette would be angry because it was not the first time. So, I lied and told her I would pay the mortgage with my check and she could use her check to pay for all of the other household bills. My thought was to find another job before she knew I was unemployed, and she would not know the mortgage payments weren't paid. Every morning, for several months, I pretended to go to work and I would apply for various jobs but wasn't hired. This added to my increased feelings of failure. At the same time, Yvette's career was improving, and she was getting promotions and recognition. The enemy used that to cause more feelings of shame; hatred began building in my heart and mind. Once the house fell into foreclosure, she found out and things were completely out of control. I felt like leaving was my only option. I moved out of the state and didn't tell my wife where I was going and would not answer anyone's calls. The devil convinced me that she was the enemy and that she was always "fault finding" and disrespecting me. I thought if I could get away, things would get better because, after all, I really thought Yvette was the problem. I could not see what the enemy was doing, and his lies became my reality. I honestly never wanted or thought we would get back together. My heart had hardened toward her and God. I was lost and I didn't even know it. Even when I was gone, God was trying to get my attention. My goal was to take as many drugs as possible or drink enough alcohol to drown out God's voice. I began pursuing other women because I never expected to stay married. Many people tried to call and reached out, but I refused to answer. I had never been so "low" in my life. After many months of running, I was sitting on a farm of a friend in Kansas, high on drugs. Again, God continued to speak, and I yelled "leave me ALONE!" I literally looked around and heard, what sounded like the cows saying "GOOOO HOOOOME!" That was it for me. I threw away the drugs, poured out the alcohol, and went back to Florida. I didn't know what I was going to do because I had ruined my marriage and I didn't think it could be fixed. What I didn't know, at the time, was that Yvette had forgiven me, submitted to God and began praying and interceding for me. I did not move back into our house. I stayed with various people because I was still bound and had not truly turned my life around. It was a long process with many ups and downs before I was able to take authority over my life and to get the strength to destroy curses, break soul ties, and get delivered from bloodline demonic assignments.

I can't thank God enough for my deliverance and for my wife becoming a Helpmeet, who stood by me, changed her life, fasted, and prayed diligently for me. She prayed so hard that I started to feel her prayers. At this point, I told God I wanted to live for Him and not for myself. I didn't want to continue to hurt my wife, my family, or myself again with my destructive behaviors. I remember God asking me if I wanted to live or die. I chose to live! This was when God started to work on my heart. God softened and healed my heart, which was the beginning of my turn-around.

Gerald's Prayer

Father, thank You for delivering me from the vicious cycle of self-destruction, from drugs, pornography, alcohol, adultery, death, and hell. Lord, I thank You for delivering me from double-mindedness, arrested development, and hard heartedness. I thank you for my wife and all she sacrificed for me and our family. Thank You for Your Word that brought stability to my mind. Your Word became medicine when I felt like I wanted to backslide. Your Word healed me of the trauma that had me going through these cycles. I declare, "Who the SON sets free is free indeed. Thank God I'm free in Christ, my Lord, and Savior.

In Jesus' name, Amen.

Reflections

Have you broken the demonic cycles that have had you bound in the past?

_____
_____
_____
_____
_____
_____
_____
_____
_____
_____
_____
_____
_____
_____
_____
_____

Reflections

Chapter 5

The Turn-Around

"So produce fruit that is consistent with repentance [demonstrating new behavior that proves a change of heart, and a conscious decision to turn away from sin]."

MATTHEW 3:8 (AMP)

Slowly my head began to rise above water, and I started to breathe again.

My turn-around season was springing forth.

The turn-around was happening in my life.

As my heart began to soften, my eyes began to open as well. When I say my eyes were being opened, it was like the scales were falling off. I began to see spiritually. It was like in Acts 9:18 (AMP) when Saul regained his sight. The Bible says, "Immediately something like scales fell from Saul's eyes, and he regained his sight. Then he got up and was baptized". For the longest time, I only saw things my way and not God's way. Blinded eyes refuse help when help is needed the most. For example, I was hurting my wife by not listening to her plead for me to get help because I didn't think I needed it. I thought I was just fine until God revealed to me that I was going to die in my sin if I didn't change my ways.

My wife warned me many times that she saw death if I didn't change what I was doing. She was experiencing Ezekiel 33:9 (AMP), which says, "But if you on your part warn the wicked man to turn from his [evil] way and he does not turn from his [evil] way, he will die in his sin; but you have saved your life." I wasn't listening to anything she was saying because I was blind to what was going on. When God gave me the choice to live or die, my eyes opened. I was living Deuteronomy 30:19 (AMP) when God said, "I call heaven and earth as witnesses against you today, that I have set before you life and death, the blessing and the curse; therefore, you shall choose life so that you may live, you and your descendants." I knew it was time for a change, and I didn't know if my time was running out or not. I asked God to give me another chance to get it right. I honestly didn't know if He accepted my plea, I just wanted to make a change daily. A change that was seen with the natural eye.

The day of turn-around honestly approached me. It was here. I was sitting on the edge of the bed, reading an email from my wife. The email was titled "Who Gerald Really Is." The fact that my wife saw the good (God) in me, and not the crap I was going through or the hell I put her through, changed my life. Something came over me as I began to read the email. As I began to speak out of my mouth the things my wife had written down, something started to jump in me.

She wrote:

God said, write down who I said Gerald is... Not how he is acting, what you think or what people say, BUT what did I say! Write the vision and make it plain. Think back, meditate, remember all of the names, positions, and callings that have been prophesied over Gerald. Then listen to me and I will instruct you as to who I created him to be and I will give you a scripture to meditate on concerning it.

Gerald is a Kingdom man

Gerald is a Kingdom father and a Kingdom husband

Gerald is a minister of health and healing

Gerald has a ministry of reconciliation

Gerald is a Prophet

Gerald will lead many souls to Christ

Gerald is the flame that fires the rocket of my ministry

Gerald is an Apostolic Leader

Gerald is a Modern-Day David

Gerald is the Priest, Prophet, and King of his home

The list went on. This captivated my mind, and at that moment, through my wife's obedience, I knew it was time to go home. I was no longer going to resist the feelings of wanting to go home. I had already spent most of my time resisting the call, my family, and what others were saying to me. This was my breaking point. I couldn't run anymore. Even the people I was living with at the time said, "When are you going back home?" "You can't keep running!" This was a prophecy in itself. These words echoed in my spirit daily. My wife wrote these declarations and was led not to share them until a year later when the Holy Spirit instructed her. Timing is everything. I went home 2-3 months later. I called my wife and told her I wanted to come home. What I didn't know is that God already spoke to her that day about leaving the back door unlocked. I wanted to go home but I didn't have a key, so I called her at work. I didn't know what she would say. To my surprise, she said to go home because the back door was unlocked for me. When my wife returned home that evening, I had slept like a newborn baby. I had not felt that much peace in what seemed like years. There was something different about the house and it helped ease the anxiety I had about being back. God told my wife to treat me like I had been there the whole time and like nothing ever happened. She did just that! She changed the way she spoke to me and I felt like a King. When she would revert to her old ways, she would quickly apologize and started showing me love. She knows I am an affectionate person and although she is not naturally affectionate, she was accommodating all my needs. I thought for sure the way she was behaving was fake or wouldn't last long, but it wasn't. I saw her love for God increase and her submission to me was consistent. I knew I didn't deserve this treatment and it began to cause me to see her and God in a new way. Our trust was rebuilt and the atmosphere in our home helped me with the difficult transition of being delivered. Years of fighting, destructive and hurtful behavior became a supernatural turn-around. It definitely took time and it is an ongoing process, but this prodigal was home for good. God's grace and my wife's strength was enough to lean on through a very tough time of deliverance and reconciliation.

Turn-around is coming.

The first thing I did was ask for forgiveness for the hell I put my wife and family through. Then God removed the shame, so I could start to forgive myself. I couldn't love anyone else if I didn't learn to love myself. I hated who I was and who I became. I was far from the person God called me to be. My deliverance didn't happen overnight. I struggled to try to shake bad habits that my flesh loved. Pornography was the hardest to release; the lust had a firm grip on me. It was a stronghold because of my past and my family curses. Due to constant stress in returning to my reality, I often reverted to taking drugs to ease my mind. I had to learn to use the Word of God to replace what the enemy suggested as a "false peace". Once I understood the power of God's Word, it truly gave me the strength to turn my life around for good. I can't tell you the perverse images or cravings for drugs don't try to come back, because they do. I have the strength and knowledge now not to act on those images. I have the power to pull them down and proclaim God's Word over my life to stay free.

Since our trust was rebuilt and my wife allowed me to feel respected, I began opening up to her when I was struggling with depression, lust, and perversion. I know this had to be very difficult for her, but she made it so much easier by the way she treated and talked to me. I started calling her and talking to her when images or urges tried to pull me back. We would pray and the power of agreement broke the enemy's hold. I know she prays for me and anoints me at night because I hear her when she goes to bed. There is always going to be a battle in my mind, but I know who is winning! In the past, the enemy was getting the best of me, but now I am the winner of every battle he tries to throw my way. This is a fixed fight; we win! I am stronger and wiser; now, my life is more disciplined and pleasing to God. My turn-around has allowed me to see how far I have come and how far I have to go. I take it one day at a time and trust God to walk with me each day. I am thankful to see the progress in my relationship with God, my wife and kids, as well as the fruit of my lifestyle changes. To God be the glory!

Gerald's Prayer

Father, I thank You for removing the scales from my eyes that I may honestly know who I am in You. Thank You for delivering me from me. I bind false identity that runs through my bloodline. I thank You for the power of Your Word that brings me the strength to fight the good fight of faith daily. No longer am I seeing through scales, but I know the man who You have called out of the cave. I command all men who are bound by any addictions to come out now in the name of Jesus. I break the stronghold of addictions that has the flesh ruling the body. I renounce the negative confessions I spoke over myself, saying I can't get over this, or this is just the way I am. The devil is a liar, and the truth is not in him. I decree that I win the battle of the mind. I am more than a conqueror. I have victory over the enemy and addictions.

In Jesus' name, Amen.

Reflections

What things can you do to help your spouse get over strongholds in their life?

_____
_____
_____
_____
_____
_____
_____
_____
_____
_____
_____
_____
_____
_____
_____

Reflections

Chapter 6

Redeeming The Time

"For thus says the LORD, 'When seventy years [of exile] have been completed for Babylon, I will visit (inspect) you and keep My good promise to you, to bring you back to this place." JEREMIAH 29:10 (AMP)

God spoke to my wife and said once Gerald gets it right, I will redeem the time you both lost. Of course, this didn't happen overnight, but God is faithful to perform His Word. I still have things to work out in my life, but the promise stands. The difference now is that I am seeking God's perfect will for my life. I wanted to live for Him and not me. When I first came home, I was still dealing with lust and pornography. I was living Romans 7:15 (AMP), "For I do not understand my own actions [I am baffled and bewildered by them]. I do not practice what I want to do, but I am doing the very thing I hate [and yielding to my human nature, my worldliness--my sinful capacity]." God began to give me strategies to fight the enemy. I would read prayer and declaration books every morning. I would wake up early in the morning and walk around our house and the neighborhood for a couple of hours reading the pages He directed me to read.

I had to do it in the rain, cold, and heat. It didn't matter. God was changing my heart and my mind. There were times I didn't want to go outside in the rain and cold, and those were the times I didn't pass the test. I would fall back into old habits just that fast because I wasn't obedient or consistent with the strategy God had given me. If I wanted to keep my strength and deliverance, I needed to do the strategy every day and not just when I wanted to. Like it says in Joshua 1:8 (AMP), "This Book of the Law shall not depart from your mouth, but you shall read [and meditate on] it day and night so that you may be careful to do [everything] in accordance with all that is written in it; for then you will make your way prosperous, and then you will be successful."

I read the same prayers against addictions and strongholds often. I wanted to live and not die. I had some good days and some bad, but definitely more good.

My deliverance process was not easy. It was dirty, tiring and at times embarrassing. I had to humble myself and stay low to experience freedom and stay free. The same process I used to get delivered years ago is the same process I use today to remain free. The one thing I used to run from was the number one thing

I needed, and that was accountability. I need the accountability of my wife to help me through deliverance. Once trust was built back between my wife and me, I trusted her enough to hold me accountable. The Word of God was my daily bread. The scriptures spoke life and strength to my spirit. Fasting and prayer allowed me to starve those addictions and the lust that was plaguing me. My wife and I speak consistent declarations over our marriage and ourselves. I am also open and honest. Once I expose in the moment the thoughts and desires I struggle with, she uses her authority in spiritual warfare. God gave us the strategy to become proactive instead of reactive to the enemy's devices. We remain ready and able to deal with attacks and assignments when they arise, if needed. We are now both equipped, and our eyes are open to see from afar off. This process continues daily and we are committed to it.

As God continues to soften my heart, I am able to love my wife more and more. Our friendship has returned, and we enjoy a stronger relationship now than we did before our separations. I asked God to let me feel the pain that I caused her. But, be careful what you ask for—you might get it. I began to listen to my wife's heart and not her words to fully understand her. I now desire to please God, and He gave me a second chance to please my wife. The turn-around wasn't easy or quick, but every part of the process was worth it. God is genuinely keeping His promises toward us. He is truly blessing us and restoring everything the devil stole from us. I am in a place spiritually and naturally that I thought I could never achieve. I am a better husband and man of God. If you are reading this and feel like you can't make it, the devil is a liar. Philippians 4:3 says, "I can do all things [which He has called me to do] through Him who strengthens and empowers me [to fulfill His purpose—I am self-sufficient in Christ's sufficiency; I am ready for anything and equal to anything through Him who infuses me with inner strength and confident peace" (AMP). God is no respecter of persons. If He did it for me, He can surely do it for you. I pray it doesn't take you as long as it took me. Just believe in the power of prayer, stay in His Word, and watch the turn-around happen right before your eyes.

Gerald's Prayer

Father, I thank You for the turn-around in my life, and I know You will do it for others. I pray that You have Your hand on them as You had Your hand on me through the deliverance process. Your Word says the steps of a righteous man are ordered by You. I ask Father that You order our steps daily. Father, as we decrease, You increase until it's none of us and all of You. Father, let every husband hear the heart of their wife and every wife hear the heart of their husband. I bind all bad communication that has happened in the past that will cause them not to listen. I bind the running man spirit that causes a man to run from hard conversations and problems. I decree that all husbands will stand up and be the Priest, Prophet, and King that God has called them to be and every Helpmeet would be suitable. No more delaying God's perfect will.

In Jesus' name, Amen.

Reflections

Pray and ask God for the strategy to help you overcome all assignments of the enemy.

_____

_____

_____

_____

_____

_____

_____

_____

_____

_____

_____

_____

_____

_____

_____

Reflections

Chapter 7

Living Life On the Path God Chose From The Beginning

"For you have need of patient endurance [to bear up under difficult circumstances without compromising], so that when you have carried out the will of God, you may receive and enjoy to the full what is promised." HEBREWS 10:36 (AMP)

In 2016, God asked us to move from Florida to Georgia, Most of our family lived in Florida, but God said to me I am moving you away from people, places and things of familiarity. I didn't know what that meant at the time. We loved Florida and our family, but we love God more. One night we were at a church service, and a Man of God called my wife and me up to the front of the church to give us a Word from the Lord. He said, "God wants to know, will you go?" He said this about four or five times, with this serious look on his face that said God is serious about your moving and that He has plans for us. We have had many powerful words spoken over our lives before, but this time was different. He was asking us to leave everything that we knew to move to a place where we didn't know anyone, so I thought. We looked at each other and said, "Yes." At the time, my wife was a school administrator and had worked for a school district for 25 plus years. She was making good money and her career was going very well. I was working as a personal trainer and was happy to be doing something I found rewarding. If we moved, we would be letting it all go. I was scared because I didn't want to mess things up as I had in the past. This move didn't happen overnight. But other things started to happen also. When we told God yes, heaven and earth began to shift things on our behalf for our good.

Opportunities that we didn't think were going to happen began to open.

About ten years earlier, we had an opportunity to work with Derek Prince Ministries, but at the time, my lifestyle didn't line up with the assignment. After my deliverance, the same opportunity presented itself again, and I was in a place spiritually that I could maximize the opportunity. It has allowed us to meet some wonderful people in the body of Christ. As we traveled to many different conferences around the country, God started to reveal His plan for the move.

Psalms 37:34 says, "Wait on the Lord, and keep His way, and He shall exalt thee to inherit the land: when the wicked are cut off, thou shalt see it" (AMP).

In a vision, God told me to look for the initials KSU. My first thought was Kansas State University but that isn't in Georgia and I knew God was instructing us to move between Atlanta and Dalton Georgia. So, I started to look up schools in Georgia and came across a school with those initials and found Kennesaw State University. It is in Kennesaw, Georgia. I never heard of the school or the town, but it was in between Atlanta and Dalton, Georgia. I told my wife what God said and I began to research the school. I was a football coach, and I thought maybe I would be able to coach there. The school had just begun their football program three years before. My wife and I started looking at schools she could work for in that district. She had an interview in the first week she applied, felt she did well in the interview, but God had another plan for us.

As 2016 started to end, we decided to sell the house. God made it clear to us that we were trying to figure things out, but He was increasing our faith. We did not hear any instructions beyond moving to Georgia. We wanted information but God was not releasing any more details until we actually moved. Now, I'm going to keep it real. I told God if the house sold before the year was up, we will move. If you have ever sold your home, you know it takes some time for people to look at the house and for paperwork to be complete. We were headed to Atlanta for a conference in early December. Before we left, I called a friend who had just received his real estate license and asked him to come over and talk about the sale of our house. This was the first house he would sell. I just knew it was going to take a while for the house to sell. As we talked, my friend said, "Gerald, this house is going to sell fast." I looked at him and said, "Man, this is your first house, how would you know how long it's going to take." He laughed at me and started to do the paperwork. Now here I go again trying God. I told him the price we wanted, and I thought it would be too high, and that I would have to come down on the price. But God! We did this on a Monday the week of the conference. We left for the conference on a Wednesday. He called me on Thursday and asked if someone could come and look at the house. I told him we weren't there, and we didn't know if the house was clean because we left our son home and who knew how it looked. He said they can look around the outside. I said, "Sure, go ahead." Friday evening, he called again and asked when will we be home because he has someone persistent about buying the house. I reminded him that we hadn't even put a sign out in front of the house yet. How could this be happening? Then I remembered what I asked God.

Be careful what you say to God.

When we came home later Saturday night, the realtor left a message saying the people would like to see the house on Sunday. Who looks at a house on Sunday? I told him whoever looks at this house on Sunday has it. That Sunday evening, a couple came by to look at the house. They loved it! God was doing His thing, but on top of that, He showed us so much favor with all the details of the move. The couple that bought the house were pastors. That was a blessing in itself because we loved our neighbors. They were good to us, and I didn't want anyone messing up the neighborhood. Within two weeks, our house was sold, and the paperwork was done before 2017. On top of that, we received the amount we asked for. God kept His promises to us, and we had to keep our promise to Him. We moved out the first week of January. We moved in with my wife's father while our youngest daughter and my wife finished the school year. At the end of July, we moved to Georgia, not having a place to live or jobs, but trusting that God would work things out.

The move was about us being faithful to what He asked us to do. It was a hard place to be in when things weren't going as we planned. The sale of the house was smooth; the transition from moving from Florida to Georgia was good. Once we got to Georgia our faith was truly tested. For five weeks, we lived in a hotel while trying to find a house. Doubt tried to creep in, but God spoke louder. He started to give us strategies for looking for a house. We promised Him we would give Him the glory for everything, including the house. He told us what to look for and He led us to an amazing home. This didn't come without some hardship. The house is perfect for what God called us to do. Now, we are in a place where God is restoring everything the devil stole.

We had no idea that God was calling us to begin a marriage ministry. He asked us to share our testimony online and we had no idea so many people shared similar struggles to ours. Our instructions were to be honest and transparent about everything. That was not easy for either one of us, but we committed to it. My wife has a Masters Degree in counseling and through our experience and her degree, we began counseling and the ministry continued to grow. We have multiple streams of revenue with different businesses. True to His Word, we are now living the life God intended for us to live and believing Him for any increase as we continue to help others build and restore their marriage. How great is our God?

Reflections

Has God ever asked you to do something in faith that stretched you beyond your comfort level?

_____
_____
_____
_____
_____
_____
_____
_____
_____
_____
_____
_____
_____
_____
_____

Reflections

Gerald's Prayer

Father, Thank You for Your promises to us. You have been faithful to us through this journey. Lord, it hasn't been easy, but we know You had a plan all along. Thank You for giving us strength when we were weak. Father, You have shown Yourself mighty to us, and we are forever grateful for the life You have given us. We say yes to any and everything You ask us to do. We know that this walk is not about us, it's about You. Thank You for choosing us to be an example of Your love through our marriage. Father, we know You are at work in other marriages as we stand in the gap. Lord, Thank You for loving and trusting us with the lives of others. We are Your humble servants.

In Jesus' name, Amen.

LETTER TO HELPMEETS
✣
YVETTE BENTON

Why Helpmeets Fight?

A Letter to Helpmeets

Dear Helpmeet,

You are God's chosen one. There is a war in the spirit against our husbands and family, and the enemy does not want us to win.

He doesn't want us to pray.

He knows that prayer is one of our greatest weapons against him and his kingdom.

So we must pray and continue to move forward in the will of God to fulfill all that God has called us to. We cannot let him stop us. We cancel the assignment of the enemy, and we are coming to battle and we are coming to fight. There is an attack on the family and a demonic assignment to destroy the family unit. There is a war against marriages and what God is trying to do on the earth. We cannot sit by and be passive or ignorant of Satan's devices.

This is a time to get active and fight the good fight of faith.

God is preparing us and giving us the strategies, we need to keep pressing. It may be difficult for us at times, but nothing is too hard for God. The Lord is our solid Rock that cannot be moved. God is teaching his children how to be strong in Him so if there is a situation or circumstance in our midst, we must stand. Psalm 144:1 declares, "Blessed be the Lord, my Rock and my great strength, who trains my hands for war and my fingers for battle" (AMP). We must believe and understand what this scripture truly means: God is our Rock and strength. God will strategically train us in this battle to win. The kingdom suffers violence and the violent take it by force (Matthew 11:12). There is a force that is necessary to be a Helpmeet Suitable. We must be battle-ready! We will take blows periodically, and they will hurt, but we must remember that God is our Rock. We will stand and through Him we can do all things!

The enemy wants to deceive us in believing that he is not real, but indeed we have a true enemy whose assignment is, "to kill, steal, and destroy" (John 10:10). We can't just cover our heads to avoid the hits and run, because no matter where we run, the battle is still coming after you and your family.

What we don't deal with in our generational bloodline will still be bound by curses. If we don't deal with it, our children will have to. Helpmeets, let's battle! God has entrusted our hands with the battle to fight. Let's not allow our circumstances to make us feel sorry for ourselves. We have to look at the enemy and let him know we see the demonic assignment, and we are ready to war on behalf of our Priest, Prophet and King (PPK) and our children. I am ready to war on behalf of my King, are you?

When it comes to the assignments launched against our husbands, we must pray daily and cancel the assignment of the enemy. God is teaching us how to put on the whole armor of God correctly. For Ephesians 6:10-17 declares:

Be strong in the Lord [draw your strength from Him and be empowered through your union with Him] and in the power of His [boundless] might. Put on the full armor of God [for His precepts are like the splendid armor of a heavily-armed soldier], so that you may be able to [successfully] stand up against all the schemes and the strategies and the deceits of the devil. For our struggle is not against flesh and blood [contending only with physical opponents], but against the rulers, against the powers, against the world forces of this [present] darkness, against the spiritual forces of wickedness in the heavenly (supernatural) places. Therefore, put on the complete armor of God, so that you will be able to [successfully] resist and stand your ground in the evil day [of danger], and having done everything [that the crisis demands], to stand firm [in your place, fully prepared, immovable, victorious]. So stand firm and hold your ground, having tightened the wide band of truth (personal integrity, moral courage) around your waist and having put on the breastplate of righteousness (an upright heart), and having strapped on your feet the gospel of peace in preparation [to face the enemy with firm-footed stability and the readiness produced by the good news]. Above all, lift up the [protective] shield of faith with which you can extinguish all the flaming arrows of the evil one. And take the helmet of salvation, and the sword of the Spirit, which is the Word of God (AMP).

Today, God is raising up a shield in the name of Jesus. We have a shield of faith, and we refuse to allow the fiery darts of the enemy to hinder our families. There is no assignment of the enemy that is going to succeed if it's up to the Helpmeet Suitable. The sword that we carry can divide things that try to come against our King. As Helpmeets Suitable, we must refuse to allow our emotions to hinder what we know God has called us to do on the earth. When the enemy shoots darts at our family, we must remain strong in the Lord and in position to fight. We must raise up our shield, and the darts will boomerang. Every fiery dart will go back to the pit of hell where it belongs. We have to refuse to break, and the armor of God will help us continually win battle after battle and ultimately the war.

As you read my husband Gerald's story of deliverance,

freedom, and restoration, please know it was possible through God's grace and because God trained me to be a Helpmeet Suitable and to war and fight on my husband's behalf. Without the obedience of my "yes" and the strength God gave me to heal and remain faithful, I honestly couldn't tell you where my husband would be. God saved and healed us both through the leading of the Holy Spirit and obedience to His instructions. I know it may be hard, but you are a Helpmeet Suitable and you can fight and take your family back, if needed. God has given us strategies, as His secret weapons, and wisdom on how to fight and win. God would not ask us to do something that we could not do through Him. We will not be weak warriors, we are strong in the Lord.

Helpmeet, I have one question for you: Are you Suitable? We have a war to win.

In Christ,

Yvette

Reflections

What do you need to be delivered from in order to fight the good fight of faith?

_____
_____
_____
_____
_____
_____
_____
_____
_____
_____
_____
_____
_____
_____
_____
_____

Reflections

Help

☙

Insert From Help For The Helpmeet

Introduction

For years, women have been asking, "Where are all the good men?" Let me respond by saying, "Where are all the good Helpmeets?"

If you're already married, then being a Helpmeet is one of your most important assignments. If you are not married and desire to be married, then your future Husband is looking for you. Future Helpmeets should be actively preparing themselves by studying the role and healing from past hurts. There are hundreds of books, articles, podcasts, videos, tapes, workbooks, and magazines on weddings, being a bride or wife. You name it, it's out there. Unfortunately, there are limited resources available to uncover the job and responsibilities of a Helpmeet. This book will walk you through what the role of a Helpmeet entails. Although families, churches, and communities rarely discuss it, being a Helpmeet is a role God takes very seriously. Through the journey of deliverance for both me, my husband, and our marriage, I made a vow to both God and my husband to be more than just a wife. Anybody can be a wife, but it takes a submitted and obedient woman with specialized training to be a Helpmeet suitable.

By no means am I the perfect Helpmeet, but because God gave me the job, I work hard at what I do. Teaching about the role and responsibilities of a Helpmeet was birthed from the pain, frustration, and revelation of a tough time in my marriage. It was refined when I was counseling and praying with women who were believing in God for their Husbands, future Husbands, marriages, and families. I am happy to serve in this capacity because I know what the revelation has done for my marriage. As my husband and I tell the world about how good God is, we had to share our testimony. God not only delivered my Husband from lust and perversion, drugs, and deception, plus so much more, He delivered me from anger, bitterness, forgiveness, and being judgmental. Through this journey, I learned that it wasn't my job to judge but to be the Helpmeet God created for my Husband. I pray my pain has a purpose, and marriages can be saved and restored through revelation and wisdom imparted from the Holy Spirit.

Chapter 1:

I Want To Be A Helpmeet In The Beginning

Now the Lord God said, "It is not good (sufficient, satisfactory) that the man should be alone; I will make him a helper meet (suitable, adaptable, and complementary for him." Genesis 2:18 (AMPC)

"In the beginning, God created the heavens and the earth" (Genesis 1:1). It was soon after creation that God created man. After designing the man, God saw fit to create the woman out of the man. As I studied chapter 2 of Genesis, it was eye-opening to read that God called everything "good" until He created Adam. In Genesis 2:18, God said, "It is not good (sufficient, satisfactory) that the man should be alone; I will make him a helper meet (suitable, adaptable, and complementary) for him." In this verse, we see that God saw a need, and He met that need by creating a helper for Adam. This helper had to complement Adam before God would call him "good." It is out of the character of God to leave what he created in need, so He formed the woman to balance and complete

Adam. I thought to myself, "This is such a monumental task!" A task that God was so pleased with, it was impressed upon my heart to study to show myself approved for such an assignment.

As I continued to study, I asked myself, "Am I suitable? Am I adaptable? Am I complementary?" I realized that I had to be truthful with myself, and I could not decide if I was suitable, adaptable, or complementary. Therefore, I not only needed to seek God for answers, but I also asked my husband how I was doing in these areas. Consequently, it is vital to pursue God and our Husband's feedback on an ongoing basis to determine whether we are suitable and fit as his Helpmeet. As Helpmeets, we need to ask God if we are suitable for the season our Husband is currently in life, for as we go through different seasons, our needs and desires shift. When I initially asked God how I was doing as my Husband's Helpmeet, I was shocked to hear His answer. It was during a tough time in our marriage when I blamed my Husband for what we were going through. I felt like I couldn't do any better as a wife. Honestly, I was fulfilling my role as a wife, but was it the role of a Helpmeet? I honored my commitment, remained faithful, cooked, cleaned, was a good mother, and had a great career. As far as I was concerned, my husband was fortunate to have me. Sounds prideful, right? But this was truly my thinking. So you can see why I was shocked to hear God's answer to what I thought was "good." I began, and I was willing and in a place to listen. I heard a very different response from Him. Reality hit me in the face. I was wrong. God was not pleased with the way "I" was doing things. He had a different description as to what a Helpmeet suitable for my Husband was to look like. The Holy Spirit became my teacher, and I learned my role as Helpmeet. I was to respect my husband, help him in areas he needed help, and to love him unconditionally, with the love of God. No matter how he acted.

YES, you read that right.

This concept was new to me, just as it may be new to you. I had no idea what God was about to do in me and through me. I just knew God was going to deal with my Husband. Nope! He wanted to work with me.

Suitable, Adaptable, and Complementary

According to the Oxford dictionary, the word *suitable* means right or appropriate for a person, purpose, or situation. The definition of *adaptable* is to be able to adjust to new conditions and able to be modified for a new use or purpose. *Complementary* means to be combining in such a way as to enhance or emphasize the qualities of another. After reading these definitions, what comes to your mind? A Helpmeet! You are correct.

A Helpmeet must learn these terms and know how to operate

in these very attributes. Although a difficult task, it is very critical. This very task is one that often takes us out of our comfort zone. What if your Husband needs something today that he has never needed before? What will you do in a situation like this? Being in daily communion with the Holy Spirit is imperative. Why? Because the Holy Spirit is the one you who teaches and leads you in unknown seasons that you may not have seen before. When God was dealing with me regarding this very topic, the Holy Spirit said, "You're the helper." The Helpmeet is the representative of the Holy Spirit in your marriage union.

For those who are unmarried, I encourage you to study the Holy Spirit, ask Him into communion with you. Allow the Holy Spirit to prepare you to be a representative for Him. Current Helpmeets—ask God for forgiveness for doing it your way and ask Him to show you His way. Ask God to show you ways to be suitable, adaptable, and complementary to your Husband.

Reflections

What has God revealed to you about YOU that could stand in the way of your marriage being all it could be?

_____
_____
_____
_____
_____
_____
_____
_____
_____
_____
_____
_____
_____
_____
_____

Reflections

Chapter 2

Helpmeet The Hardest Job With No Training

You Got the Job!

B eing a Helpmeet is the hardest job any wife can obtain with no training, so training class is now in session! While reading this book, the Holy Spirit will begin to give you the training you need to be a suitable Helpmeet. Like any job, you can't do it well until you have the proper training and an instructor to teach it. Through my journey, God equipped me to teach this subject head-on. Now I can impart this revelation and information into others, and it is an honor. My understanding of the Helpmeet role was entirely different when I first got married. I thought saying "I do" and having a Husband were all the qualifications I needed to do my job correctly as a Helpmeet. Can I tell you, it's a lot more to this role than we think!

Why is the role of the Helpmeet so hard to grasp in the society we live in? The Helpmeet is a Kingdom principle. It does not look like what we see on television. It does not look like what we have wished for as a child. It's not that simple—it takes work. We get discouraged because the marriage we thought was going to be a fairytale turned out to be more like a circus. There are no fairytale marriages. This does not mean that marriage can't be exciting and blissful. It doesn't mean that our spouses are not going to show love, but what it does mean is that we have a responsibility to do it God's way regardless of the situation or circumstances.

The role of the Helpmeet is so crucial that training should start way before saying "I do." Unfortunately, it is usually during turmoil or in counseling sessions that we come to the realization that we have not done what was needed to prepare or handle such a monumental task.

There is a rise in women in ministry, women in business, and women in key roles in our country. However, this does not mean that God has not called us to be submissive in our homes. God is using women in a compelling way, and it's not stopping anytime soon. The Chayil woman is on the rise as a woman of strength. In Hebrew, *Chayil* means one that is anointed with strength, wisdom, virtue, power, wealth, and might. Women are being used mightily in ministry, and miracles, signs, and wonders are happening. Prophecies are being fulfilled at this very moment. We saw it in some of the 2018 elections, and we're seeing it happen in the body of Christ. However, this is not changing the Word of God about what women are to do in our homes and with our Husbands. If we don't get our assignment in order, we are going to miss out on what God is doing in our lives. We could miss out on important blessings and instructions from God because we are out of order in our homes. We must operate within the divine order of God so we are able to do what He has called for us to do in His Kingdom.

God is a lot of things, but He is not a God of chaos. He is a God of order, and He does not change his mind. So, if you're called to be married, even if you're separated, and God has told you to work on your marriage relationship, then you must fight for your family. If you're standing in the gap or have a Husband that's not entirely delivered, don't give up on him or your destiny. Isaiah 55:11 (AMPC) declares, "So shall My Word be that goes forth out of My mouth: it shall not return to Me void [without producing any effect, useless], but it shall accomplish that which I please and purpose, and it shall prosper in the things for which I sent it." Stand on the Word of God and do what He has instructed of you. If we want God's Word to produce results, we must live our lives according to it. As Helpmeets, we must become knowledgeable of principles and strategies concerning our role moving forward. I will describe these in the upcoming chapters.

Submission is also an important topic and is a key characteristic of a Helpmeet. Submission is a form of respect and humility. God clearly expects Helpmeets to be submitted to their Husbands. This is a difficult task for many women that are leaders. There is a biblical way to bring God into your household and make things happen, change, and improve. Respect and honor must be intentional if we are to meet our biblical responsibilities as a Helpmeet. I will admit, I did not know how to accomplish this as a strong woman. I knew how to make things happen in my workplace and church. When the enemy came into my home, I had to be consistent with the strategies God told me to put in place. I commanded the enemy to leave my home because I know my role and authority.

When I learned how to submit to my husband, I also learned how to respect him, regardless of what he did. I know it's hard to believe I said, "Whatever he does," but it will become more apparent as you read further. For example, God may have called you into ministry, but it seems that God is unconcerned that your Husband may not be saved, needs deliverance, or is not following through with his role as a Husband. Trust me, there is hope because nothing is impossible through Christ. There was a time my husband was on drugs, and God asked me to stand in the gap and intercede for him while being in ministry. I may not have respected his behavior or what he was doing, but God's

Word commanded that I respect him. Once we make up our minds and line ourselves with the Word of God, we can expect God to step in. When God steps in, He can do the miraculous.

Did I believe this could happen at first? No, but I believe it now because I witnessed it. When I stepped out of the way, and got quiet before the Lord, and was submitted, I watched God snatch my Husband from the hands of the enemy. I experienced God heal me, and it allowed me to grow spiritually because I moved out of God's way. As you read through these next few pages, ask yourself this question: What is God's job description of a Helpmeet?

Are You Ready for the Job?

Helpmeets assist, come beside their Husbands, and complete them. It is a role that requires much prayer and time with God, as well as an obedient heart. God bless our mothers, but they may not have had a lot of training or understanding of a Helpmeet. Others may not have had parents that were married. Therefore, we may not have had an example of a Helpmeet growing up. Often, we look to leaders in our society, our culture, and/or in the church, but we do not necessarily see a true Godly example of Kingdom marriage. Instead, we're seeing what people have become comfortable with and have become complacent in marriage.

As I've studied the Helpmeet role, what I saw and thought was right was not necessarily what God ordered. When I petitioned God, I saw in my own life that I was not lining up with God's Word. I asked God in prayer what he meant by asking me to be a Helpmeet suitable. I thought to myself, I'm home every day, I go to church, I'm saved, and I have a career. Basically, I thought I was a Proverbs 31 woman, but that was not enough for the warfare I was experiencing in my home. God said, "Yvette, you need to be the Helpmeet that Gerald needs. There are specific things that he needs, and if you allow me, I will help you become suitable." Do you know, I was extremely offended? Let me be transparent. When God responded, I asked, "What do you mean? I told God, I do this, I do that, I do more than what I think some other people do." The Lord told me, "But I need you to be suitable, and that means whatever your Husband needs. I placed what you needed in you before you were placed in your mother's womb because I knew you would be with him. I created you to be with him, and there are some strategic tools that I have inside of you to help him accomplish his purpose. However, you are not using them properly, and one of those tools is being a Helpmeet suitable."

God also impressed upon me the importance of being submitted and how to follow and encourage my husband to lead. God taught me, if he's doing this, be quiet. If he's doing that, pray for him. If he's not acting right, continue to do as God directs. So many people thought I was crazy, but truthfully, I was obedient. According to Genesis 2:21, we come from the side of the man. We are a part of our Husbands and have been called alongside them. Some may ask what to do if their Husband never gets saved or never changes? What if he never does, right? Does God still expect me to do all this? When I asked the same questions, God reminded me of the sacrifice of Jesus. He said, "I asked my son Jesus to give up his life. I am asking you to sacrifice as well." I realized it was like Jesus asking God why He should have to give up His life without the guarantee that everyone would be saved and choose to serve Him. Of course, Jesus did not say that. Christ knew He wanted to please the Father and declared He would give up His will for the will of the Father. To fulfill His destiny, it did not matter whether one person or several million people got saved, Jesus knew He was to do what the Father asked of Him.

If you are not willing to put in the work or you are looking for an easy way out, being a Helpmeet suitable will not be possible. We must trust and understand that the Word of God works, and it will not return void. Therefore, it is imperative that your life lines up with the Word for you to have the power through God to accomplish becoming suitable. God expects us to be the example of His Word. Allow God to use you for His glory in your home and allow your spouse to see, feel, and hear God through you. We must renew our minds to realize that no matter what our spouse does, God will only hold us accountable for our actions. Our focus is to hear our Master say, "Well done, good and faithful servant" (Matthew 25:23, AMP).

In Proverbs 18:21 (AMPC), the Bible says, "Death and life are in the power of the tongue, and they who indulge in it shall eat of it [for death or life]." Because you have a covenant with your Husband, you can speak life into him and cause the atmosphere in your home to change. Until his deliverance comes, and you see a manifestation of your prayers, be an example of a living epistle of obedience. Pray for him and show him the Agape love of God unconditionally.

If you are ready for the job of a Helpmeet and want to continue your journey and training, order your copy of the entire book and workbook *Help For The Helpmeet*. God wants you equipped for the journey that He has assigned you to. You can order a copy from our website at geraldandyvette.com or on Amazon.

Reflections

What is needed for you to be a Helpmeet Suitable or a Priest, Prophet and King?

_____
_____
_____
_____
_____
_____
_____
_____
_____
_____
_____
_____
_____
_____
_____
_____

Reflections

RESTORATION

Chapters 1

Restoration Is Possible

We were excited to begin our marriage ministry and God told us that we would provide help and hope to those in need. I (Yvette) would provide help, and Gerald would provide hope. On this journey, God has been so good to us that we can't keep it to ourselves. It is the mandate of God that this book is released and sent forth for what it was created to do. We have seen the restoration of God firsthand and want to release restoration over marriages and individuals who are believing God for the same. We have been through so much in our marriage. God made a promise to restore it all back, but restoration takes work, discipline, and consistency. God is not a respecter of persons; if He did it for us, He most certainly will do it for you.

One of the ways God was faithful to us in the restoration process was restoring the family unit. We have been asked in the past: What about the children? What happened to the children through the hardships in our marriage, and how did it affect them? Especially concerning the separation, lust, and perversion. This is an area that we continue to pray heavily about. It was the hardest for the youngest because she was home when the worse of the discord started to take place. I would say often, "Pray for your dad. I don't know how, but God is going to work it out." The children asked questions all the time. There was a time we put a tracker on Gerald's phone so our daughter could see her dad's location, when she could not talk to him. We prayed that God would protect and bless them through the deliverance and restoration process. Through the process, we had to be respectful of the children, especially our adult children, and not share a lot until they were ready. God has done the miraculous for our entire family. Many don't know, but it wasn't until years after our restoration that we recently took a family vacation for the first time. It was breathtaking to see the fulfillment of God's promises to us. We have prayed, toiled, asked, and begged God for all that is unfolding before our very eyes. In the manifestation of our family restoration, we are watching the children hug, giggle, and talk to each other. What a joy it brings to our hearts for Gerald to be in his place as the King over our home. Gerald has had to work extremely hard to rebuild the relationships with our children. It is an ongoing endeavor, but he is diligent. We know that God is a rewarder of those that diligently seek Him, and we seek Him continuously about our entire family restoration.

If God did it for us, He can definitely do it for you. We know what it looks like, what it sounds like, what it feels like in the beginning, middle, and right at the point of breakthrough. In the middle of the process, we don't know what God will do, but we have to go through it. God wants to show His glory to the world through marriages. He is using ours, and He will use yours. Let this be a testimony of God's grace to push you to keep going. The reward of walking through the process is the restoration of everything. God is giving it all back to you, just like He is doing for us.

God can and will restore. Get the help that you need to get yourself in the right place emotionally for this journey. It is a very tough process, we won't sugar-coat it, but we would do it all over again knowing what we know now. We tell couples and individuals to be diligent.

Diligent may not feel good.

Diligent may seem odd.

Diligent will cause other people to talk about you, but do it anyway.

The process of restoration started with healing for me and deliverance for Gerald. He had to get delivered, maintain his deliverance, which in turn started the restoration process. The process of deliverance looked like this:

I believed God for my healing and studied to show myself approved as a Helpmeet. I changed what I could personally do and trusted that a sanctified wife could sanctify a husband. Gerald asked for forgiveness, started going to church again, and allowed God to hold him accountable. Gerald began to ask God and me for help and prayer with any struggles openly. He worked on one struggle/addiction at a time. The process of deliverance got easier, but it was still work. Prayer, fasting, and strategic declarations and decrees are key. Through the process of deliverance, we continued to believe God for full restoration. We can never forget that God is able and through Him all things are possible.

As we ponder on the goodness of Jesus, we can't help but think—God is worthy of the praise that is due Him. When thinking through the process of praying, praising, and worshipping the one true living God, we see that God is truly able! Looking at the past and where God has brought us now is mind-blowing. If you are going through trials, tests, and tribulations, you wonder will God truly work it out. Yes, He can work it out, but it won't usually be the way we think it should or the timing we may want it. No matter what it looks like, don't give up on anything God has asked you to do!

We have to plow and continue to sow seeds of faith. The enemy will try his best to sow seeds of discord, doubt, and confusion, but we have to stand on the Word of God and keep moving. God is able to do anything and everything. Nothing is too hard for God. Ephesians 3:20-21 states, "Now to Him Who, by (in consequence of) the [action of His] power that is at work within us, is able to [carry out His purpose and] do superabundantly, far over *and* above all that we [dare] ask or think [infinitely beyond our highest prayers, desires, thoughts, hopes, or dreams]—To Him be glory in the church and in Christ Jesus throughout all generations forever and ever. Amen" (AMPC). This is not a cliché, but the truth. We cannot allow difficult moments to alter our future promises from manifesting. We must continue to ask, seek, and knock until the door is opened (Matthew 7:7-12).

The words that we speak must line up with the Word of God. Negative talk should not come out of our mouth. Our reality should be only to say words that produce power and give life. Our actions must line up with what we speak as well. As kingdom citizens, we must pray and shut down the thoughts that make us feel like God is not able. God is an undefeated God; we must remember that God is on our side. He wants us to win. We must decree and declare daily that God is able.

In the process of restoration, God wants to change our

mindsets. He wants us to have a renewed mind to walk in His promises. He wants us to enjoy what we worked so hard for. God sees the sacrifices of His people and loves to reward. We must ask the Holy Spirit for strength to keep going. God has the power to change our situation at any time. We must believe this with all our heart. To fight the good fight of faith, we must do it spiritually. We must die to our flesh daily to remain strong through the process.

The process is definitely ordained by God. Thank you for taking this journey with us. It was a pleasure to share our Help and Hope journey with you. Remember, if God can do it for us, He can do it for you!

Restoration Prayer

Father, in the name of Jesus, thank You for doing exceedingly abundantly above all that we can ask or think. Father, we ask for forgiveness for giving up on You. We ask for forgiveness for not doing the things that You have asked us to do from the beginning. Father, we come to You fully submitted with a humble heart, surrendering all that we have to You. We commit to doing things Your way and not ours. Father, we no longer try to walk by our flesh, but by Your Spirit. Father, renew our mind. Let this mind be in us that is also in Christ Jesus. In the name of Jesus, we break every curse that has caused us to fall back. We bind all forms of memory recall that bring us back to our past and traumatic experiences in our lives.

In the name of Jesus, we come against that spirit of quitting that causes us to consider giving up.

You have not given us a spirit of fear, but of power, love, and a sound mind. Please give us the strength we need to walk this walk with You daily. We come against every mind-hindering spirit. Father, remove every scale off our eyes now so that we may truly see You for who You are. Lord, increase our spiritual discernment and insight. Break down every wall that blocks us from our deliverance and from getting close to You. Lord, remove all limitations from our lives so that we may completely serve You.

Father, we know all things are possible through You in the name of Jesus. Increase our faith to go higher in You. We rely entirely on You. God; Your word is a lamp unto our feet and a light unto our pathway. We decree and declare that Your light shines in every dark area of our lives. Father, search our hearts and see if there is anything in us that is not like You. We hunger and thirst after righteousness. Thank You, Lord, for giving Your only begotten Son to die on the cross and pay the price for our sins. We have been forgiven by You; therefore, we can forgive ourselves and others. Thank You for giving us the strength to remain in this faith walk.

Father, no matter who has traumatized us, misled us, or mistreated us, we forgive them. We release them now in the name of Jesus and speak a blessing over their lives. Father, we cancel every negative word spoken over us and our lives. Father, forgive us for operating out of our emotions. Now that our hearts and minds are clear, please give us the strength to fight for and the wisdom to heal marriages. Bring every marriage into a new place of peace in You. We speak restoration over marriages right now in the name of Jesus. Take every marriage to a great place in You. We speak new romance, new intimacy, and a divine connection like never before. Father, let unions experience the true covenant of God. We come against every covenant-breaking spirit and every marriage-breaking spirit now in the name of Jesus. We declare that You are hiding marriages under Your wing. We declare that marriages will live in harmony, peace, and experience joy. We break all forms of disorder, disunity, and dysfunctional communication. Father, restore, reset, and reboot all marriages. We speak a hedge of protection around marriages and homes.

Father, nothing is impossible with You. Father, we speak healing and deliverance over every marriage. In Jesus' name, breathe life into every dead marriage and we say ARISE! God, we know that You are no respecter of persons, and You desire for all Your people to be whole. We declare hope and wholeness over marriages. We thank You for bringing help in many forms in the name of Jesus. God, we thank You for the resources that are coming to marriages. We bind every spirit of backlash and retaliation. We thank You, Lord, that You have called us victorious. We are not victims, and we break the victim mentality. We have victory over our minds and triumph over the enemy. We declare that the enemy is under our feet.

We are winners!

We are more than conquerors in the name of Jesus!

We walk in total victory!

Father, allow all marriages to gain wisdom, knowledge, and understanding. We come against all forms of death, hell, and the grave that has been trying to kill, steal, and destroy marriage relationships, destiny, and purpose. We cancel the assignment now in the name of Jesus. Release every family from the hand of the enemy. Married couples and individuals will dream again. Father, thank You for healing all infirmity, sickness, and disease. By Your stripes, we are completely healed physically and emotionally. Father, we declare Your healing power now in the name of Jesus. We release the power of the blood. We declare the power of the blood over marriages. We thank You, Lord, for bringing marriages into right alignment with You.

Father, in the name of Jesus, we break all forms of addictions and generational curses that try to destroy marriages. We come against alcohol abuse, verbal abuse, mental abuse, and spiritual abuse now in the name of Jesus. We bind rejection, bitterness and abandonment and replace them with love, adoption and peace. Father, fill every void of hurt with Your love and rekindle our love for You. Father, thank You for pitching tents over our homes to protect us from all danger, all forms of accidents and incidents. We declare angels are dispatched on our behalf to cover and protect. Thank You, Lord, that we are generational curse breakers and we break all forms of ungodliness over our lives, marriages, and children.

We cancel all spirits of divorce and separation and decree marriages are unifying supernaturally. All assignments of adultery and perversion are reversed, and the spirit of the strange man and the strange women is severed. We use our sword of the spirit to cut all ungodly soul ties. We break the back of the prodigal assignment that the enemy is using to divide households. We speak to every prodigal and declare you are coming home, and the home is conducive for deliverance, reconciliation, and peace.

Every married couple is studying to show themselves approved in their marriage roles as the Priest, Prophet and King (PPK) and a Helpmeet Suitable. We declare what God has joined together let no man put asunder. We decree the restoration power of God and believe you are restoring marriages supernaturally! The two shall become one!

Now, in the name of Jesus, Father, we shift the atmosphere over our homes, communities, and our territory. We declare now that Your kingdom come and Your will be done on earth as it is in heaven.

We break every curse.

We break every old mindset.

We break old habits.

We break old speech.

We break old perspectives.

We break old hearing.

We break away from everything that will cause us to slip and fall.

Every trap and snare that has been set for us, we break it and declare it will come down now in the name of Jesus.

We thank You, Father, that all things are possible through You. Please give us the strength to change our declarations and our words to align with Your will for our lives. We praise You, Lord, that the nation will experience and see the restoration of marriages. Father, we restore purity back to marriages through the blood of Jesus. May the grace of God be on those that have experienced restoration to speak up in boldness and be used for God's glory to bring restoration to the Kingdom of God. We may be bent, but we are not broken. Thank You, Lord, that HELP AND HOPE is our portion.

IN JESUS MIGHTY NAME, AMEN.

Reflections

Write a personal prayer canceling your own generational curses or hindrances.

_____
_____
_____
_____
_____
_____
_____
_____
_____
_____
_____
_____
_____
_____
_____
_____

Reflections

Contact Gerald & Yvette Benton

Contact Gerald and Yvette Benton on their various social media platforms:

Facebook: @Yvette Benton, @Gerald Benton

Instagram: @GeraldandYvette

Twitter: @GeraldandYvette

Website: www.GeraldandYvette.com

Email: Geraldandyvette@gmail.com

www.ingramcontent.com/pod-product-compliance
Lightning Source LLC
Chambersburg PA
CBHW070052120426
42742CB00048B/2479